An Adult Coloring Book Celebrating Natural Hair

by Unicia R. Buster

Enjoy your Coloring!

Copyright
Copyright ©2016 by Unicia R. Buster
All rights reserved.

International Standard Book Number
ISBN-13: 978-1539637967
ISBN-10: 1539637964

Manufactured in the United States

Printed by CreateSpace
www.CreateSpace.com/ColoringCurls
Available from Amazon.com and other retail outlets

"Embrace what makes you unique, even if it makes others uncomfortable."

~ Janelle Monae

"Be bold. Be brave enough to be your true self."
~ Queen Latifah

*"I am not my hair. I am not this skin.
I am the soul that lives within."*

~ India Arie

*"Everything you want to be, you already are.
You're simply on the path to discovering it."*

~ Alicia Keys

"You've got to be happy in your own skin."
~ Jada Pinkett Smith

*"Whipping your hair means
not being afraid to be yourself."*

~ Willow Smith

"No matter who you are, no matter where you come from, you are beautiful."

~ Michelle Obama

"If you are always trying to be normal, you will never know how amazing you can be."

~ Maya Angelou

"It is both humiliating and humbling to discover that a single generation after the events that constructed me as a public personality, I am remembered as a hairdo."

~ Angela Davis

"The most common way people give up their power is by thinking they don't have any."

~ Alice Walker

"There is no paycheck that can equal the feeling of contentment that comes from being the person you are meant to be."

~ Oprah Winfrey

"If you focus more on the inside, you'll feel just as great about the outside. I feel attractive when I'm doing good and helping people."

~ Keke Palmer

*"The only thing worse than being blind
is having sight but no vision."*

~ Helen Keller

"The most alluring thing a woman can have is confidence."

~ Beyoncé Knowles

"I consider myself a crayon… I may not be your favorite color but one day you'll need me to complete your picture."

~ Lauryn Hill

"If you want to fly, you have to give up the things that weigh you down."

~ Toni Morrison

"I am an expression of the divine... I have a right to be this way...I can't apologize for that, nor can I change it, nor do I want to."

~ Alice Walker

*"Every freckle on my face is where it's supposed to be,
and I know my creator didn't make no mistakes on me.
My feet, my thighs, my lips, my eyes
– I'm loving what I see."*

~ India Arie

"You can wear all the greatest clothes and all the greatest shoes, but you've got to have a good spirit on the inside. That's what's really going to make you look like you're ready to rock the world."

~ Alicia Keys

*"My hair is an aesthetic choice…
At the same time, how you wear your hair
is a political statement as well."*

~ Erykah Badu

*"Beauty is about enhancing what you have.
Let yourself shine through."*

~ Janelle Monae

"You don't need another person, place or thing to make you whole. God already did that. Your job is to know it."

~ Maya Angelou

"The reality is, I like imperfection. You take away from the world when you're not yourself. Whatever is unique and special about you was designed by God."

~ Queen Latifah

*"I want to embrace my full self,
as natural as I can be."*

~ Willow Smith

"Precious jewel, you glow, you shine, reflecting all the good things in the world. Just look at yourself."

~ Maya Angelou

"It's time that women truly owned their superpowers and used their beauty and strength to change the world around them."

~ Janelle Monae

"Breathing is meditation; life is a meditation. You have to breathe in order to live, so breathing is how you get in touch with the sacred space of your heart."

~ Willow Smith

*"I'm no longer accepting the things I cannot change…
I'm changing the things I cannot accept."*

~ Angela Davis

*"Whenever you are creating beauty around you,
you are restoring your own soul."*

~ Alice Walker

"The minute you settle for less than you deserve, you get even less than you settled for."

~ Kimora Lee Simmons

A special thank you to God, my mom, Teresa, my aunt, Juanita, and my son, Adrian, for your continuous support. I love you.

And a very special thank you to Dionne, Julia, Adepero, Shana, Tsedey, Bria, Clifton, Jordyn, Kyle, and Aurora for allowing me to capture your beauty on these pages.

~ Unicia R. Buster

Made in the USA
Middletown, DE
23 December 2016